Muhlenberg County Libraries
117 S. Main
Greenville, Kentucky 42345

DATE DUE

Stars
and Planets

Angela Royston

Illustrated by
Stephen Maturin
and Roger Stewart

Heinemann Interactive Library
Des Plaines, Illinois

Contents

©1998 Reed Educational & Professional Publishing
Published by Heinemann Interactive Library,
an imprint of Reed Educational & Professional Publishing,
1350 East Touhy Avenue, Suite 240 West
Des Plaines, IL 60018

Printed and bound in Italy. See-through pages printed by SMIC, France.

02 01 00 99 98
10 9 8 7 6 5 4 3 2 1

Library of Congress Cataloging in Publication Data
Royston, Angela.
    Stars and planets / Angela Royston; illustrated by Stephen Maturin.
        p.   cm. — (Inside and out)
    Includes bibliographical references and index.
    Summary: Text and captioned illustrations present information
about the stars, sun, moon, and the planets.
    ISBN 1-57572-182-1 (library binding)
    1. Astronomy—Juvenile literature.   [1. Astronomy.]   I. Maturin,
Stephen, ill.   II. Title.   III. Series.
QB46.R69   1998
520—dc21   97-42625
                                                                   CIP
                                                                   AC

Acknowledgments
The Publishers would like to thank the following for permission to reproduce photographs: page 8: David Shayler © NASA;
page 11 top right: Tom Bean © Tony Stone Images; page 13: Jerry Schad © Science Photo Library; pages 14, 16, 18 and 21: Science Photo Library
© NASA; page 15: Pekka Paviainen © Science Photo Library; page 17: © ZEFA; page 19: Kevin Kelley © Tony Stone Images.

Some words are shown in bold, **like this.**
You can find out what they mean by looking in the glossary.

The Sky at Night

When you look up at the night sky, you might see the moon and millions of twinkling lights. These lights are coming from stars that are billions of miles away. Each star is actually a far away **sun**.

Sometimes you can see bright lights that move quickly across the sky. These often belong to aircraft that are landing nearby. Can you see the aircraft in the picture on the left?

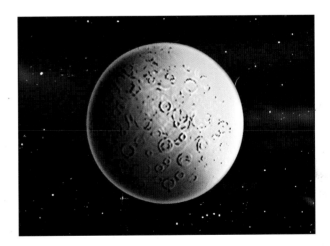

The moon is the biggest object in the night sky. It looks bigger than the stars because it is much closer.

The Stars

For thousands of years, people have looked at the stars. They noticed how some groups of stars always looked the same. They connected these stars with imaginary lines to make shapes and gave them names. The group on the right is called Orion the Hunter.

Groups of stars are called constellations. The constellation on the right is called The Big Dipper.

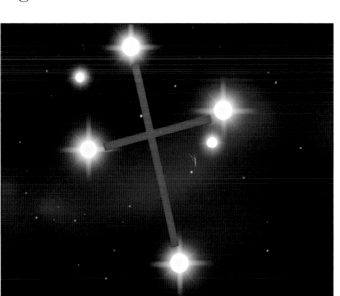

On the left is The Southern Cross. It can only be seen from south of the **equator**.

Looking Closer

Telescopes make things that are far away look closer and much bigger. Scientists use them to study stars. The biggest telescopes are often built in special **observatories** at the top of mountains. There, the air is clear and the stars are easier to see.

The Hubble telescope flies around the earth in **space**. Flying high above the clouds, it can see the stars more clearly than telescopes on Earth.

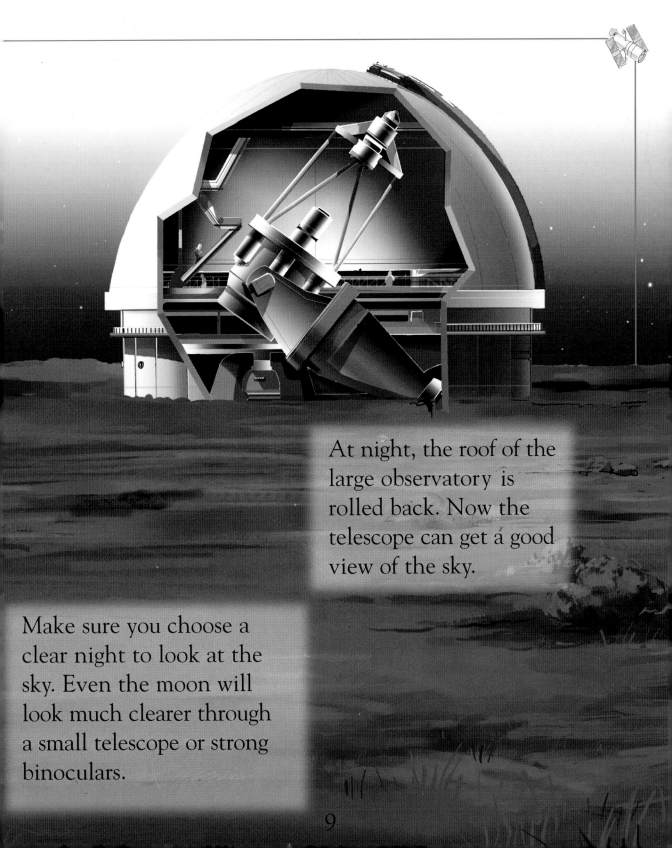

At night, the roof of the large observatory is rolled back. Now the telescope can get a good view of the sky.

Make sure you choose a clear night to look at the sky. Even the moon will look much clearer through a small telescope or strong binoculars.

Shooting Stars

Some objects look like they have long tails. These are comets. Comets are balls of ice and dust that move across the sky. Halley's Comet flies close to the earth every 76 years. Most comets appear less often.

This **crater** in Arizona was made thousands of years ago by a meteorite. Meteorites are big chunks of rock that fall to Earth from **space.**

Sometimes small pieces of space rocks burn up as they fall to Earth. These are shooting stars. Shooting stars flash across the sky. Don't blink or you will miss them!

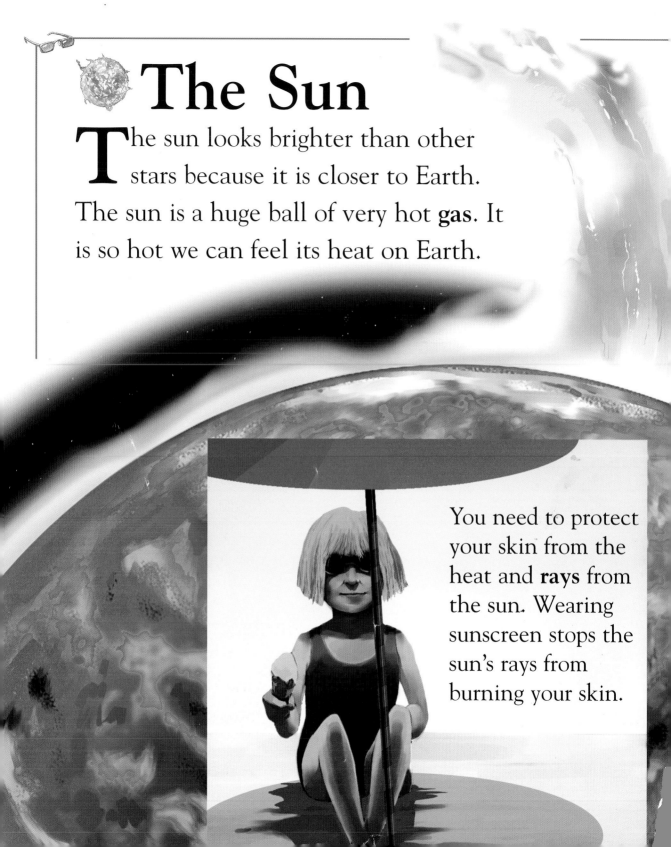

The Sun

The sun looks brighter than other stars because it is closer to Earth. The sun is a huge ball of very hot **gas**. It is so hot we can feel its heat on Earth.

You need to protect your skin from the heat and **rays** from the sun. Wearing sunscreen stops the sun's rays from burning your skin.

The light from behind these trees is the first sign that a new day is beginning. Daylight is light from the sun. It is so bright it will block out the light from other stars.

The earth is like a huge spinning ball. As it spins, it moves around the sun. The side of the earth that faces the sun is in daylight. The other side is in darkness.

The Planets

Earth is just one of nine planets that travels around the **sun.** Each planet is really much further from the sun than it looks in this picture. Scientists use **telescopes** and space probes to find out what the planets are like.

b

a

a. Pluto
b. Neptune
c. Uranus
d. Saturn
e. Jupiter

f. Mars
g. Earth
h. Venus
i. Mercury

In 1997, the space probe *Pathfinder* landed on Mars. It carried the *Sojourner* vehicle. This little buggy had cameras that took pictures of Mars' surface.

g

i

f

h

d

e

c

You can see other planets
from Earth. The bright light
next to the moon is Venus.
It is sometimes called the
Evening Star because it is
often the first to appear at
night.

The Moon

The moon is a huge rock that circles the earth. In 1969, the first **astronauts** landed there. The moon has no air, so the astronauts wore special suits and took oxygen with them to breathe.

This is what the earth looks like from the moon. It is surrounded by clouds. Unlike Earth, the moon does not have clouds, life, or water.

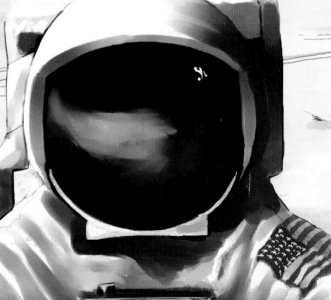

When the astronauts landed on the moon, they took many photographs. They collected moon rocks and brought them back to Earth.

No one has landed on the moon since 1972. Astronauts left behind American flags, landing capsules, and even a space buggy that was used to explore the surface.

Can you see the footprints in the dust? There is no wind to blow them away.

 Rocky Planets

Mercury, Venus, and Mars are rocky planets like Earth. Their surfaces are covered with **craters** and mountains. **Astronauts** have never visited them, but space probes have. This probe landed on Mars before *Pathfinder* (page 14) and explored the planet. It found that Mars has no water and is very cold.

Mercury is the closest planet to the **sun.** The craters on its surface have been made by meteorites crashing into it.

Venus is surrounded by thick, poisonous orange clouds. The ground is so hot, no astronaut can ever land there.

Living in Space

Will people ever live on the moon or on Mars? Scientists have already designed special stations like this one. People can live and work inside the domes.

In space there is no **gravity** to keep one's feet on the ground. **Astronauts** float about instead.

Metals could be mined from the planet's soil and spacecraft would take the metal back to Earth.

Inside the domes are homes, offices, and a medical center. Plants could be grown inside for food and to keep the air fresh.

Outer Planets

The outer planets—Jupiter, Saturn, Uranus, Neptune, and Pluto—are large balls of **gas** and liquid. Can you see a red spot on Jupiter, the largest planet? It is made by big whirling storm clouds.

Jupiter

Uranus

Pluto is the only planet that the space probe, **Voyager 2,** did not travel past. Pluto is so far away, it takes almost 250 years for it to circle the **sun.** It only takes the earth one **year**!

Neptune

Pluto

Pluto has one moon (below) that is almost as big as Pluto itself.

Saturn

23

Glossary

astronaut	person who travels in space
crater	hole in the ground made by an explosion
equator	imaginary line around the middle of the earth
gas	substance that is neither solid nor liquid
gravity	force that pulls you towards the ground
observatories	special buildings that have telescopes and other instruments to study stars and planets
ray	beam of light
space	empty distance between planets and stars
sun	huge, hot, glowing ball of gas
telescope	tool that uses lenses and mirrors to make far away objects look closer
Voyager 2	space probe launched in 1977, that traveled past the outer planets (except Pluto) by 1989
year	length of time it takes the earth to go around the sun

More books to read

Brodie, Caroline. *The Planets: Neighbors in Space.* Brookfield, Conn: Millbrook Press, 1991.

Packard, Mary. *Stars and Planets.* Mahwah, NJ: Troll Communications, 1995.

Rosen, Sidney. *How Far Is a Star?* Minneapolis, Minn: Lerner Publishing Group, 1992.

Index